## THIS JOURNAL BELONGS TO:

Susie Hou

If found, please contact me:

email -

tel -

social -

100 Day Money Mindset Journal ™

Copyright © 2020. www.nelsonsoh.com

ISBN: 9798674216223

# 100
## DAY
## MONEY
## MINDSET
## JOURNAL

*Unlock your unlimited potential
to attact money into your life.*

当你的余额能匹配你对生活的野心和向往.

并且符合你的眼界和层次. 多少钱啊?

# HOW TO GET
# THE MOST
## OUT OF THIS JOURNAL:

**1** DEDICATE 100
DAYS OF EFFORT.
This journal takes 5 minutes a day.
You have the time.

**2** BE REALISTIC AND
HONEST WITH
YOURSELF.
Set yourself up for the best
chance of success.

**3** TURN YOUR PLANS
INTO ACTIONS.
Execute on your plans,.
Don't just stare at them.

# PROGRESS

1 2 3 4 5 6 7

8 9 10 11 12 13 14

15 16 17 18 19 20 21

22 23 24 25 26 27 28

29 30 31 32 33 34 35

36 37 38 39 40 41 42

43 44 45 46 47 48 49

# TRACKER

50 51 52 53 54 55 56

57 58 59 60 61 62 63

64 65 66 67 68 69 70

71 72 73 74 75 76 77

78 79 80 81 82 83 84

85 86 87 88 89 90 91

92 93 94 95 96 97 98

99 100

# WEEK 1
# KICK-OFF

"I fear not the man who has practiced 10,000 kicks once, but I fear the man who has practiced one kick 10,000 times."
-Bruce Lee

# WEEKLY GOALS

### Goal #1

New balance : $500

I am saving for    6 months of emergency funds (Saving Acct.)

How much I need to save: $3000 × 6 = $18 000

How will I reach my goal?   Saving $800 bi-weekly. ($1600)

   11 months will allow me to reach goal

### Goal #2

New balance $11000

I am saving for   Investment chicken.

How much I need to save:   $. 20,000

How will I reach my goal?   Save $600 bi-weekly (1200)

   17 months will allow me to reach goal

### Goal #3

I am saving for   房车

How much I need to save:   $70,000.

How will I reach my goal?  Second job .

Goal #4  Master school.       Goal #5  Travel the world

   $ 40,000.  Third job...             $100,000

"A journey of
a thousand miles
must begin with
a single step."

LAO TZU

# DAY 1

**DATE:** 2021. 11. 28

In one word, I feel: _Lucky_

I am grateful for: _peaceful time_

Today's money affirmation statement:

_I will spend less than I earn_

## How I will work towards my weekly goals:

Goal #1: _Clear Credit card debt_

Goal #2: _Finding second income source_

Goal #3: _Saving for emergency Fund Pool_

---

**Daily checklist:**

- [ ] Review bank accounts
- [ ] Review credit cards
- [ ] Pay bills that are due
- [ ] Review payments due this week
- [ ] _____

---

## What did I spend money on today?

|  | Need | Want |
|---|---|---|
| _Bought $50 on gift for 积衣114_ | ✓ | ☐ |
|  | ☐ | ☐ |
|  | ☐ | ☐ |
|  | ☐ | ☐ |
|  | ☐ | ☐ |

Money is abundant and there is more than enough to go around.

Notes

# DAY 2

**DATE:**

In one word, I feel:

I am grateful for:

Today's money affirmation statement:

How I will work towards my weekly goals:

Goal #1:

Goal #2:

Goal #3:

Daily checklist:

☐ Review bank accounts    ☐ Review payments due this week

☐ Review credit cards

☐ Pay bills that are due    ☐

What did I spend money on today?

                 Need     Want

☐    ☐

☐    ☐

☐    ☐

☐    ☐

☐    ☐

# "Never spend your money before you have it."

THOMAS JEFFERSON

# DAY 3

**DATE:** _____

In one word, I feel: _____

I am grateful for: _____

Today's money affirmation statement:

_____

How I will work towards my weekly goals:

Goal #1: _____

Goal #2: _____

Goal #3: _____

Daily checklist:

☐ Review bank accounts      ☐ Review payments due this week

☐ Review credit cards

☐ Pay bills that are due      ☐ _____

What did I spend money on today?

|  | Need | Want |
|---|---|---|
| _____ | ☐ | ☐ |
| _____ | ☐ | ☐ |
| _____ | ☐ | ☐ |
| _____ | ☐ | ☐ |
| _____ | ☐ | ☐ |

"A WISE PERSON
SHOULD HAVE MONEY
IN THEIR HEAD,
BUT NOT IN
THEIR HEART."

JONATHAN SWIFT

Notes

# DAY 4

**DATE:** _____

In one word, I feel: _____

I am grateful for: _____

Today's money affirmation statement:

_____

How I will work towards my weekly goals:

Goal #1: _____

Goal #2: _____

Goal #3: _____

---

Daily checklist:

☐ Review bank accounts          ☐ Review payments due
                                          this week
☐ Review credit cards
                                ☐ _____
☐ Pay bills that are due

---

What did I spend money on today?

|  | Need | Want |
|---|---|---|
| _____ | ☐ | ☐ |
| _____ | ☐ | ☐ |
| _____ | ☐ | ☐ |
| _____ | ☐ | ☐ |
| _____ | ☐ | ☐ |

*"Wealth consists not in having great possessions, but in having few wants."*

EPICTETUS

Notes

# DAY 5

**DATE:**

In one word, I feel:

I am grateful for:

Today's money affirmation statement:

How I will work towards my weekly goals:

Goal #1:

Goal #2:

Goal #3:

Daily checklist:

☐ Review bank accounts    ☐ Review payments due this week

☐ Review credit cards

☐ Pay bills that are due    ☐ _____

What did I spend money on today?

| | Need | Want |
|---|---|---|
| | ☐ | ☐ |
| | ☐ | ☐ |
| | ☐ | ☐ |
| | ☐ | ☐ |
| | ☐ | ☐ |

*I am capable of earning more income.*

# DAY 6

**DATE:** _____

In one word, I feel: _____

I am grateful for: _____

Today's money affirmation statement:

_____

How I will work towards my weekly goals:

Goal #1: _____

Goal #2: _____

Goal #3: _____

---

Daily checklist:

☐ Review bank accounts      ☐ Review payments due
☐ Review credit cards           this week
☐ Pay bills that are due      ☐ _____

---

What did I spend money on today?

|  | Need | Want |
|---|---|---|
| _____ | ☐ | ☐ |
| _____ | ☐ | ☐ |
| _____ | ☐ | ☐ |
| _____ | ☐ | ☐ |
| _____ | ☐ | ☐ |

# "Rule No. 1:
# Never lose money.

# Rule No. 2:
# Never forget Rule No. 1."

WARREN BUFFETT

Notes

# DAY 7

**DATE:** _____

In one word, I feel: _____

I am grateful for: _____

Today's money affirmation statement:

_____

How I will work towards my weekly goals:

Goal #1: _____

Goal #2: _____

Goal #3: _____

Daily checklist:

☐ Review bank accounts    ☐ Review payments due this week

☐ Review credit cards

☐ Pay bills that are due    ☐ _____

What did I spend money on today?

|  | Need | Want |
|---|---|---|
| _____ | ☐ | ☐ |
| _____ | ☐ | ☐ |
| _____ | ☐ | ☐ |
| _____ | ☐ | ☐ |
| _____ | ☐ | ☐ |

# 10 MINUTE WEEKLY
# SELF - REFLECTION

In general, this week I feel:

Why do I feel this way?

What can I do next week to feel great?

# SELF - REFLECTION:  WEEK 1

This week I am the MOST grateful for:

_____

Something great that happened to me this week:

_____

How I feel about money this week:

😟 ◯ ◯ ◯ ◯ 😐 ◯ ◯ ◯ ◯ 😄

Why do I feel this way?

_____

_____

_____

What can I do next week to feel great about money?

_____

_____

_____

# WEEK 2
# CAN'T STOP
# WON'T STOP

*"The biggest adventure you can ever take is to live the life of your dreams."*

OPRAH WINFREY

# WEEKLY GOALS

## Goal #1

I am saving for _____

How much I need to save: _____

How will I reach my goal? _____

_____

## Goal #2

I am saving for _____

How much I need to save: _____

How will I reach my goal? _____

_____

## Goal #3

I am saving for _____

How much I need to save: _____

How will I reach my goal? _____

_____

Everyday I am becoming
richer and richer.

Notes

# DAY 8

**DATE:** _____

In one word, I feel: _____

I am grateful for: _____

Today's money affirmation statement:

_____

How I will work towards my weekly goals:

Goal #1: _____

Goal #2: _____

Goal #3: _____

---

Daily checklist:

☐ Review bank accounts     ☐ Review payments due this week

☐ Review credit cards

☐ Pay bills that are due     ☐ _____

---

What did I spend money on today?

|  | Need | Want |
|---|---|---|
| _____ | ☐ | ☐ |
| _____ | ☐ | ☐ |
| _____ | ☐ | ☐ |
| _____ | ☐ | ☐ |
| _____ | ☐ | ☐ |

"If you wish to get rich, save what you get. A fool can earn money, but it takes a wise man to save and dispose of it to his own advantage."

BRIGHAM YOUNG

Notes

# DAY 9

**DATE:**

In one word, I feel:

I am grateful for:

Today's money affirmation statement:

How I will work towards my weekly goals:

Goal #1:

Goal #2:

Goal #3:

---

Daily checklist:

☐ Review bank accounts
☐ Review credit cards
☐ Pay bills that are due
☐ Review payments due this week
☐ _____

---

What did I spend money on today?

|  | Need | Want |
|---|---|---|
|  | ☐ | ☐ |
|  | ☐ | ☐ |
|  | ☐ | ☐ |
|  | ☐ | ☐ |
|  | ☐ | ☐ |

*"It takes as much energy to wish as it does to plan."*

Eleanor Roosevelt

Notes
_____
_____
_____
_____
_____
_____
_____

# DAY 10

**DATE:** _____

In one word, I feel: _____

I am grateful for: _____

Today's money affirmation statement:

_____

How I will work towards my weekly goals:

Goal #1: _____

Goal #2: _____

Goal #3: _____

---

Daily checklist:

☐ Review bank accounts          ☐ Review payments due this week

☐ Review credit cards

☐ Pay bills that are due         ☐ _____

---

What did I spend money on today?

|  | Need | Want |
|---|---|---|
| _____ | ☐ | ☐ |
| _____ | ☐ | ☐ |
| _____ | ☐ | ☐ |
| _____ | ☐ | ☐ |
| _____ | ☐ | ☐ |

I can create my own
wealth and prosperity.

Notes

# DAY 11

**DATE:** _____

In one word, I feel: _____

I am grateful for: _____

Today's money affirmation statement:

_____

How I will work towards my weekly goals:

Goal #1: _____

Goal #2: _____

Goal #3: _____

Daily checklist:

☐ Review bank accounts          ☐ Review payments due
☐ Review credit cards               this week
☐ Pay bills that are due           ☐ _____

What did I spend money on today?

| | Need | Want |
|---|---|---|
| _____ | ☐ | ☐ |
| _____ | ☐ | ☐ |
| _____ | ☐ | ☐ |
| _____ | ☐ | ☐ |
| _____ | ☐ | ☐ |

*Every great teacher who has ever walked the planet has told you that life was meant to be abundant.*

**James Ray**

Notes

# DAY 12

**DATE:**

In one word, I feel: _____

I am grateful for: _____

Today's money affirmation statement:

_____

How I will work towards my weekly goals:

Goal #1: _____

Goal #2: _____

Goal #3: _____

Daily checklist:

- [ ] Review bank accounts
- [ ] Review credit cards
- [ ] Pay bills that are due
- [ ] Review payments due this week
- [ ] _____

What did I spend money on today?

|  | Need | Want |
| --- | --- | --- |
| _____ | [ ] | [ ] |
| _____ | [ ] | [ ] |
| _____ | [ ] | [ ] |
| _____ | [ ] | [ ] |
| _____ | [ ] | [ ] |

# OTHERS HAVE DONE IT, AND I CAN TOO.

Notes

# DAY 13

**DATE:** _____

In one word, I feel: _____

I am grateful for: _____

Today's money affirmation statement:

_____

How I will work towards my weekly goals:

Goal #1: _____

Goal #2: _____

Goal #3: _____

---

Daily checklist:

☐ Review bank accounts          ☐ Review payments due
☐ Review credit cards              this week
☐ Pay bills that are due          ☐ _____

---

What did I spend money on today?

|  | Need | Want |
|---|---|---|
| _____ | ☐ | ☐ |
| _____ | ☐ | ☐ |
| _____ | ☐ | ☐ |
| _____ | ☐ | ☐ |
| _____ | ☐ | ☐ |

"A penny saved is
a penny earned."

BENJAMIN FRANKLIN

Notes

# DAY 14

**DATE:** _____

In one word, I feel: _____

I am grateful for: _____

Today's money affirmation statement:

_____

How I will work towards my weekly goals:

Goal #1: _____

Goal #2: _____

Goal #3: _____

---

Daily checklist:

☐ Review bank accounts  ☐ Review payments due
☐ Review credit cards        this week
☐ Pay bills that are due  ☐ _____

---

What did I spend money on today?

|  | Need | Want |
|---|---|---|
| _____ | ☐ | ☐ |
| _____ | ☐ | ☐ |
| _____ | ☐ | ☐ |
| _____ | ☐ | ☐ |
| _____ | ☐ | ☐ |

# 10 MINUTE WEEKLY SELF - REFLECTION

In general, this week I feel:

😕 ◯ ◯ ◯ ◯ 😐 ◯ ◯ ◯ ◯ 😁

Why do I feel this way?

_____

_____

_____

What can I do next week to feel great?

_____

_____

_____

# SELF - REFLECTION:  WEEK 2

This week I am the MOST grateful for:

_____

Something great that happened to me this week:

_____

How I feel about money this week:

◉ ○ ○ ○ ○ ◉ ○ ○ ○ ○ ◉

Why do I feel this way?

_____

_____

_____

What can I do next week to feel great about money?

_____

_____

_____

# WEEK 3
# UPWARDS

*"Screw it. Let's do it!"*

RICHARD BRANSON

# WEEKLY GOALS

### Goal #1

I am saving for _____

How much I need to save: _____

How will I reach my goal? _____

_____

### Goal #2

I am saving for _____

How much I need to save: _____

How will I reach my goal? _____

_____

### Goal #3

I am saving for _____

How much I need to save: _____

How will I reach my goal? _____

_____

"How many millionaires do you know who have become wealthy by investing in savings accounts?
I rest my case."

ROBERT G. ALLEN

Notes

# DAY 15

**DATE:** _____

In one word, I feel: _____

I am grateful for: _____

Today's money affirmation statement:

_____

How I will work towards my weekly goals:

Goal #1: _____

Goal #2: _____

Goal #3: _____

## Daily checklist:

☐ Review bank accounts    ☐ Review payments due this week

☐ Review credit cards

☐ Pay bills that are due    ☐ _____

## What did I spend money on today?

| | Need | Want |
|---|---|---|
| _____ | ☐ | ☐ |
| _____ | ☐ | ☐ |
| _____ | ☐ | ☐ |
| _____ | ☐ | ☐ |
| _____ | ☐ | ☐ |

# I welcome wealth into my life from all angles.

Notes

# DAY 16

**DATE:**

In one word, I feel:

I am grateful for:

Today's money affirmation statement:

How I will work towards my weekly goals:

Goal #1:

Goal #2:

Goal #3:

Daily checklist:

- [ ] Review bank accounts
- [ ] Review credit cards
- [ ] Pay bills that are due
- [ ] Review payments due this week
- [ ]

What did I spend money on today?

| | Need | Want |
|---|---|---|
| | [ ] | [ ] |
| | [ ] | [ ] |
| | [ ] | [ ] |
| | [ ] | [ ] |
| | [ ] | [ ] |

# "Believe you can and you're halfway there."

## THEODORE ROOSEVELT

Notes

# DAY 17

**DATE:** _____

In one word, I feel: _____

I am grateful for: _____

Today's money affirmation statement:

_____

How I will work towards my weekly goals:

Goal #1: _____

Goal #2: _____

Goal #3: _____

Daily checklist:

☐ Review bank accounts       ☐ Review payments due
☐ Review credit cards             this week
☐ Pay bills that are due         ☐ _____

## What did I spend money on today?

|  | Need | Want |
|---|---|---|
| _____ | ☐ | ☐ |
| _____ | ☐ | ☐ |
| _____ | ☐ | ☐ |
| _____ | ☐ | ☐ |
| _____ | ☐ | ☐ |

"We make a living
by what we get,
but we make a life
by what we give."

**WINSTON CHURCHILL**

Notes

_____

_____

_____

_____

_____

_____

_____

_____

# DAY 18

**DATE:** _____

In one word, I feel: _____

I am grateful for: _____

Today's money affirmation statement:

_____

How I will work towards my weekly goals:

Goal #1: _____

Goal #2: _____

Goal #3: _____

---

Daily checklist:

☐ Review bank accounts    ☐ Review payments due this week

☐ Review credit cards

☐ Pay bills that are due    ☐ _____

---

What did I spend money on today?

| | Need | Want |
|---|---|---|
| _____ | ☐ | ☐ |
| _____ | ☐ | ☐ |
| _____ | ☐ | ☐ |
| _____ | ☐ | ☐ |
| _____ | ☐ | ☐ |

# Money flows freely to me.

# DAY 19

**DATE:**

In one word, I feel:

I am grateful for:

Today's money affirmation statement:

How I will work towards my weekly goals:

Goal #1:

Goal #2:

Goal #3:

Daily checklist:

- [ ] Review bank accounts
- [ ] Review credit cards
- [ ] Pay bills that are due
- [ ] Review payments due this week
- [ ]

What did I spend money on today?

|  | Need | Want |
|---|---|---|
|  | [ ] | [ ] |
|  | [ ] | [ ] |
|  | [ ] | [ ] |
|  | [ ] | [ ] |
|  | [ ] | [ ] |

# I am grateful for all the money that has flowed in and out of my life.

Notes

# DAY 20

**DATE:** _____

In one word, I feel: _____

I am grateful for: _____

Today's money affirmation statement:

_____

How I will work towards my weekly goals:

Goal #1: _____

Goal #2: _____

Goal #3: _____

Daily checklist:

☐ Review bank accounts

☐ Review credit cards

☐ Pay bills that are due

☐ Review payments due this week

☐ _____

What did I spend money on today?

| | Need | Want |
|---|---|---|
| _____ | ☐ | ☐ |
| _____ | ☐ | ☐ |
| _____ | ☐ | ☐ |
| _____ | ☐ | ☐ |
| _____ | ☐ | ☐ |

"Live as if you were
to die tomorrow.
Learn as if you were
to live forever."

**MAHATMA GANDHI**

Notes

# DAY 21

**DATE:** _____

In one word, I feel: _____

I am grateful for: _____

Today's money affirmation statement:

_____

How I will work towards my weekly goals:

Goal #1: _____

Goal #2: _____

Goal #3: _____

---

**Daily checklist:**

☐ Review bank accounts     ☐ Review payments due this week

☐ Review credit cards

☐ Pay bills that are due     ☐ _____

---

## What did I spend money on today?

| | Need | Want |
|---|---|---|
| _____ | ☐ | ☐ |
| _____ | ☐ | ☐ |
| _____ | ☐ | ☐ |
| _____ | ☐ | ☐ |
| _____ | ☐ | ☐ |

# 10 MINUTE WEEKLY SELF - REFLECTION

In general, this week I feel:

Why do I feel this way?

What can I do next week to feel great?

# SELF - REFLECTION:  WEEK 3

This week I am the MOST grateful for:

_____

Something great that happened to me this week:

_____

How I feel about money this week:

😕  ◯  ◯  ◯  ◯  😐  ◯  ◯  ◯  ◯  😁

Why do I feel this way?

_____

_____

_____

What can I do next week to feel great about money?

_____

_____

_____

# WEEK 4
## KEEP UP THE
## MOMENTUM

it's a marathon

not a sprint...

# WEEKLY GOALS

### Goal #1

I am saving for _____

How much I need to save: _____

How will I reach my goal? _____

_____

### Goal #2

I am saving for _____

How much I need to save: _____

How will I reach my goal? _____

_____

### Goal #3

I am saving for _____

How much I need to save: _____

How will I reach my goal? _____

_____

"Wealth is a mindset.
It's all about
how you think.
Money is literally
attracted to you
or repelled from you."

**DAVID SCHIRMER**

Notes

_____

_____

_____

_____

_____

_____

_____

# DAY 22

**DATE:** _____

In one word, I feel: _____

I am grateful for: _____

Today's money affirmation statement:

_____

How I will work towards my weekly goals:

Goal #1: _____

Goal #2: _____

Goal #3: _____

---

Daily checklist:

☐ Review bank accounts    ☐ Review payments due this week

☐ Review credit cards

☐ Pay bills that are due    ☐ _____

---

## What did I spend money on today?

| | Need | Want |
|---|---|---|
| _____ | ☐ | ☐ |
| _____ | ☐ | ☐ |
| _____ | ☐ | ☐ |
| _____ | ☐ | ☐ |
| _____ | ☐ | ☐ |

"Don't just make money,
make a difference."

GRANT CARDONE

# DAY 23

**DATE:** _____

In one word, I feel: _____

I am grateful for: _____

Today's money affirmation statement:

_____

How I will work towards my weekly goals:

Goal #1: _____

Goal #2: _____

Goal #3: _____

Daily checklist:

☐ Review bank accounts

☐ Review credit cards

☐ Pay bills that are due

☐ Review payments due this week

☐ _____

What did I spend money on today?

| | Need | Want |
|---|---|---|
| _____ | ☐ | ☐ |
| _____ | ☐ | ☐ |
| _____ | ☐ | ☐ |
| _____ | ☐ | ☐ |
| _____ | ☐ | ☐ |

# I will be
# the first millionaire
# in my family.

Notes

_____

_____

_____

_____

_____

_____

_____

# DAY 24

**DATE:**_____

In one word, I feel: _____

I am grateful for: _____

Today's money affirmation statement:

_____

How I will work towards my weekly goals:

Goal #1: _____

Goal #2: _____

Goal #3: _____

---

Daily checklist:

☐ Review bank accounts     ☐ Review payments due
☐ Review credit cards            this week
☐ Pay bills that are due    ☐ _____

---

What did I spend money on today?

|  | Need | Want |
|---|---|---|
| _____ | ☐ | ☐ |
| _____ | ☐ | ☐ |
| _____ | ☐ | ☐ |
| _____ | ☐ | ☐ |
| _____ | ☐ | ☐ |

"Money is a terrible master but an excellent servant."

P.T. BARNUM

Notes

# DAY 25

**DATE:** _____

In one word, I feel: _____

I am grateful for: _____

Today's money affirmation statement:

_____

How I will work towards my weekly goals:

Goal #1: _____

Goal #2: _____

Goal #3: _____

---

Daily checklist:

☐ Review bank accounts     ☐ Review payments due this week

☐ Review credit cards

☐ Pay bills that are due     ☐ _____

---

What did I spend money on today?

| | Need | Want |
|---|---|---|
| _____ | ☐ | ☐ |
| _____ | ☐ | ☐ |
| _____ | ☐ | ☐ |
| _____ | ☐ | ☐ |
| _____ | ☐ | ☐ |

# "Don't stay in bed, unless you can make money in bed."

GEORGE BURNS

Notes

# DAY 26

**DATE:** _____

In one word, I feel: _____

I am grateful for: _____

Today's money affirmation statement:

_____

How I will work towards my weekly goals:

Goal #1: _____

Goal #2: _____

Goal #3: _____

---

Daily checklist:

☐ Review bank accounts    ☐ Review payments due this week

☐ Review credit cards

☐ Pay bills that are due    ☐ _____

---

What did I spend money on today?

|  | Need | Want |
|---|---|---|
| _____ | ☐ | ☐ |
| _____ | ☐ | ☐ |
| _____ | ☐ | ☐ |
| _____ | ☐ | ☐ |
| _____ | ☐ | ☐ |

# I am in full control of my finances.

Notes

# DAY 27

**DATE:** _____

In one word, I feel: _____

I am grateful for: _____

Today's money affirmation statement:

_____

How I will work towards my weekly goals:

Goal #1: _____

Goal #2: _____

Goal #3: _____

---

Daily checklist:

☐ Review bank accounts      ☐ Review payments due
☐ Review credit cards            this week
☐ Pay bills that are due        ☐ _____

---

What did I spend money on today?

|  | Need | Want |
|---|---|---|
| _____ | ☐ | ☐ |
| _____ | ☐ | ☐ |
| _____ | ☐ | ☐ |
| _____ | ☐ | ☐ |
| _____ | ☐ | ☐ |

# I have a healthy and positive money mindset.

Notes

# DAY 28

**DATE:** _____

In one word, I feel: _____

I am grateful for: _____

Today's money affirmation statement:

_____

How I will work towards my weekly goals:

Goal #1: _____

Goal #2: _____

Goal #3: _____

Daily checklist:

☐ Review bank accounts      ☐ Review payments due
☐ Review credit cards              this week
☐ Pay bills that are due        ☐ _____

What did I spend money on today?

|  | Need | Want |
|---|---|---|
| _____ | ☐ | ☐ |
| _____ | ☐ | ☐ |
| _____ | ☐ | ☐ |
| _____ | ☐ | ☐ |
| _____ | ☐ | ☐ |

# 10 MINUTE WEEKLY SELF - REFLECTION

In general, this week I feel:

🙁 ◯ ◯ ◯ ◯ 😐 ◯ ◯ ◯ ◯ 😁

Why do I feel this way?

_____

_____

_____

What can I do next week to feel great?

_____

_____

# SELF - REFLECTION:  WEEK 4

This week I am the MOST grateful for:

_____

Something great that happened to me this week:

_____

How I feel about money this week:

😕 ◯ ◯ ◯ ◯ 😐 ◯ ◯ ◯ ◯ 😁

Why do I feel this way?

_____

_____

_____

What can I do next week to feel great about money?

_____

_____

_____

# WEEK 5
## OVER 1/4 THE
## WAY THERE!

ALL PROGRESS IS GOOD PROGRESS.

# WEEKLY GOALS

### Goal #1

I am saving for _____

How much I need to save: _____

How will I reach my goal? _____

_____

### Goal #2

I am saving for _____

How much I need to save: _____

How will I reach my goal? _____

_____

### Goal #3

I am saving for _____

How much I need to save: _____

How will I reach my goal? _____

_____

Money is not the
root to all evil.
The **LOVE** and **GREED**
for money is the
root to all evil.

Notes

# DAY 29

**DATE:** _____

In one word, I feel: _____

I am grateful for: _____

Today's money affirmation statement:

_____

How I will work towards my weekly goals:

Goal #1: _____

Goal #2: _____

Goal #3: _____

---

Daily checklist:

☐ Review bank accounts     ☐ Review payments due
☐ Review credit cards         this week
☐ Pay bills that are due     ☐ _____

---

What did I spend money on today?

|  | Need | Want |
|---|---|---|
| _____ | ☐ | ☐ |
| _____ | ☐ | ☐ |
| _____ | ☐ | ☐ |
| _____ | ☐ | ☐ |
| _____ | ☐ | ☐ |

"Twenty years from now you will be more disappointed by the things that you didn't do than by the ones you did do."

MARK TWAIN

Notes

# DAY 30

**DATE:** _____

In one word, I feel: _____

I am grateful for: _____

Today's money affirmation statement:

_____

How I will work towards my weekly goals:

Goal #1: _____

Goal #2: _____

Goal #3: _____

---

**Daily checklist:**

☐ Review bank accounts          ☐ Review payments due
☐ Review credit cards              this week
☐ Pay bills that are due          ☐ _____

---

## What did I spend money on today?

|  | Need | Want |
|---|:---:|:---:|
| _____ | ☐ | ☐ |
| _____ | ☐ | ☐ |
| _____ | ☐ | ☐ |
| _____ | ☐ | ☐ |
| _____ | ☐ | ☐ |

# I HAVE THE MINDSET OF A MULTIMILLIONAIRE.

Notes

# DAY 31

**DATE:**

In one word, I feel:

I am grateful for:

Today's money affirmation statement:

How I will work towards my weekly goals:

Goal #1:

Goal #2:

Goal #3:

## Daily checklist:

☐ Review bank accounts  ☐ Review payments due this week

☐ Review credit cards

☐ Pay bills that are due  ☐

## What did I spend money on today?

| | Need | Want |
|---|---|---|
| | ☐ | ☐ |
| | ☐ | ☐ |
| | ☐ | ☐ |
| | ☐ | ☐ |
| | ☐ | ☐ |

# I will always do my best to give money to help good causes.

# DAY 32

**DATE:** _____

In one word, I feel: _____

I am grateful for: _____

Today's money affirmation statement:

_____

How I will work towards my weekly goals:

Goal #1: _____

Goal #2: _____

Goal #3: _____

---

Daily checklist:

☐ Review bank accounts    ☐ Review payments due this week

☐ Review credit cards

☐ Pay bills that are due    ☐ _____

---

What did I spend money on today?

|  | Need | Want |
|---|---|---|
| _____ | ☐ | ☐ |
| _____ | ☐ | ☐ |
| _____ | ☐ | ☐ |
| _____ | ☐ | ☐ |
| _____ | ☐ | ☐ |

"Every time you borrow money, you're robbing your future self."

NATHAN W. MORRIS

Notes

# DAY 33

**DATE:**

In one word, I feel:

I am grateful for:

Today's money affirmation statement:

How I will work towards my weekly goals:

Goal #1:

Goal #2:

Goal #3:

---

Daily checklist:

☐ Review bank accounts
☐ Review credit cards
☐ Pay bills that are due

☐ Review payments due this week
☐ _____

---

What did I spend money on today?

| | Need | Want |
|---|---|---|
| | ☐ | ☐ |
| | ☐ | ☐ |
| | ☐ | ☐ |
| | ☐ | ☐ |
| | ☐ | ☐ |

# I support my friends and family in their financial endeavours.

Notes

# DAY 34

**DATE:** _____

In one word, I feel: _____

I am grateful for: _____

Today's money affirmation statement:

_____

How I will work towards my weekly goals:

Goal #1: _____

Goal #2: _____

Goal #3: _____

---

Daily checklist:

☐ Review bank accounts    ☐ Review payments due this week

☐ Review credit cards

☐ Pay bills that are due    ☐ _____

---

What did I spend money on today?

|  | Need | Want |
|---|---|---|
| _____ | ☐ | ☐ |
| _____ | ☐ | ☐ |
| _____ | ☐ | ☐ |
| _____ | ☐ | ☐ |
| _____ | ☐ | ☐ |

"The only place where success comes before work is in the dictionary."

*VIDAL SASSOON*

Notes

# DAY 35

**DATE:** _____

In one word, I feel: _____

I am grateful for: _____

Today's money affirmation statement:

_____

How I will work towards my weekly goals:

Goal #1: _____

Goal #2: _____

Goal #3: _____

Daily checklist:

☐ Review bank accounts
☐ Review credit cards
☐ Pay bills that are due

☐ Review payments due this week

☐ _____

What did I spend money on today?

| | Need | Want |
|---|---|---|
| _____ | ☐ | ☐ |
| _____ | ☐ | ☐ |
| _____ | ☐ | ☐ |
| _____ | ☐ | ☐ |
| _____ | ☐ | ☐ |

# 10 MINUTE WEEKLY
# SELF - REFLECTION

In general, this week I feel:

Why do I feel this way?

_____

_____

_____

What can I do next week to feel great?

_____

_____

_____

# SELF - REFLECTION:  WEEK 5

This week I am the MOST grateful for:

_____

Something great that happened to me this week:

_____

How I feel about money this week:

😦 ◯ ◯ ◯ ◯ 😐 ◯ ◯ ◯ ◯ 😁

Why do I feel this way?

_____

_____

_____

What can I do next week to feel great about money?

_____

_____

_____

# WEEK 6
## DREAMS DON'T WORK UNLESS YOU DO

# WEEKLY GOALS

## Goal #1

I am saving for _____

How much I need to save: _____

How will I reach my goal? _____

_____

## Goal #2

I am saving for _____

How much I need to save: _____

How will I reach my goal? _____

_____

## Goal #3

I am saving for _____

How much I need to save: _____

How will I reach my goal? _____

_____

"If you live for having it all, what you have is never enough."

VICKI ROBIN

Notes

# DAY 36

**DATE:**

In one word, I feel:

I am grateful for:

Today's money affirmation statement:

How I will work towards my weekly goals:

Goal #1:

Goal #2:

Goal #3:

Daily checklist:

☐ Review bank accounts
☐ Review credit cards
☐ Pay bills that are due
☐ Review payments due this week
☐

What did I spend money on today?

|  | Need | Want |
|---|---|---|
|  | ☐ | ☐ |
|  | ☐ | ☐ |
|  | ☐ | ☐ |
|  | ☐ | ☐ |
|  | ☐ | ☐ |

*I am a
money magnet.*

# DAY 37

**DATE:** _____

In one word, I feel: _____

I am grateful for: _____

Today's money affirmation statement:

_____

How I will work towards my weekly goals:

Goal #1: _____

Goal #2: _____

Goal #3: _____

Daily checklist:

- ☐ Review bank accounts
- ☐ Review credit cards
- ☐ Pay bills that are due
- ☐ Review payments due this week
- ☐ _____

What did I spend money on today?

| | Need | Want |
|---|---|---|
| _____ | ☐ | ☐ |
| _____ | ☐ | ☐ |
| _____ | ☐ | ☐ |
| _____ | ☐ | ☐ |
| _____ | ☐ | ☐ |

"The more you learn, the more you earn."

WARREN BUFFETT

Notes

# DAY 38

**DATE:** _____

In one word, I feel: _____

I am grateful for: _____

Today's money affirmation statement:

_____

How I will work towards my weekly goals:

Goal #1: _____

Goal #2: _____

Goal #3: _____

---

Daily checklist:

☐ Review bank accounts     ☐ Review payments due this week

☐ Review credit cards

☐ Pay bills that are due     ☐ _____

---

## What did I spend money on today?

|  | Need | Want |
|---|---|---|
| _____ | ☐ | ☐ |
| _____ | ☐ | ☐ |
| _____ | ☐ | ☐ |
| _____ | ☐ | ☐ |
| _____ | ☐ | ☐ |

"MANY PEOPLE TAKE NO CARE OF THEIR MONEY TILL THEY COME NEARLY TO THE END OF IT, AND OTHERS DO JUST THE SAME WITH THEIR TIME."

JOHANN WOLFGANG VON GOETHE

Notes

# DAY 39

**DATE:** _____

In one word, I feel: _____

I am grateful for: _____

Today's money affirmation statement:

_____

How I will work towards my weekly goals:

Goal #1: _____

Goal #2: _____

Goal #3: _____

---

Daily checklist:

☐ Review bank accounts        ☐ Review payments due
                                  this week
☐ Review credit cards
                              ☐ _____
☐ Pay bills that are due

---

What did I spend money on today?

|  | Need | Want |
|---|---|---|
| _____ | ☐ | ☐ |
| _____ | ☐ | ☐ |
| _____ | ☐ | ☐ |
| _____ | ☐ | ☐ |
| _____ | ☐ | ☐ |

# I will eliminate all my self-limiting beliefs around money.

# DAY 40

**DATE:** _____

In one word, I feel: _____

I am grateful for: _____

Today's money affirmation statement:

_____

How I will work towards my weekly goals:

Goal #1: _____

Goal #2: _____

Goal #3: _____

Daily checklist:

☐ Review bank accounts          ☐ Review payments due
☐ Review credit cards               this week
☐ Pay bills that are due          ☐ _____

What did I spend money on today?

|  | Need | Want |
|---|---|---|
| _____ | ☐ | ☐ |
| _____ | ☐ | ☐ |
| _____ | ☐ | ☐ |
| _____ | ☐ | ☐ |
| _____ | ☐ | ☐ |

*"When buying shares, ask yourself, would you buy the whole company?"*

Rene Rivkin

# DAY 41

**DATE:**_____

In one word, I feel: _____

I am grateful for: _____

Today's money affirmation statement:

_____

How I will work towards my weekly goals:

Goal #1: _____

Goal #2: _____

Goal #3: _____

---

Daily checklist:

☐ Review bank accounts     ☐ Review payments due this week

☐ Review credit cards

☐ Pay bills that are due     ☐ _____

---

What did I spend money on today?

|  | Need | Want |
|---|---|---|
| _____ | ☐ | ☐ |
| _____ | ☐ | ☐ |
| _____ | ☐ | ☐ |
| _____ | ☐ | ☐ |
| _____ | ☐ | ☐ |

# "Do what you love and the money will follow."

## MARSHA SINETAR

Notes

# DAY 42

**DATE:** _____

In one word, I feel: _____

I am grateful for: _____

Today's money affirmation statement:

_____

How I will work towards my weekly goals:

Goal #1: _____

Goal #2: _____

Goal #3: _____

Daily checklist:

☐ Review bank accounts
☐ Review credit cards
☐ Pay bills that are due
☐ Review payments due this week
☐ _____

What did I spend money on today?

| | Need | Want |
|---|---|---|
| _____ | ☐ | ☐ |
| _____ | ☐ | ☐ |
| _____ | ☐ | ☐ |
| _____ | ☐ | ☐ |
| _____ | ☐ | ☐ |

# 10 MINUTE WEEKLY SELF - REFLECTION

In general, this week I feel:

Why do I feel this way?

_____

_____

_____

What can I do next week to feel great?

_____

_____

_____

# SELF - REFLECTION:  WEEK 6

This week I am the MOST grateful for:

_____

Something great that happened to me this week:

_____

How I feel about money this week:

😕 ○ ○ ○ ○ 😐 ○ ○ ○ ○ 😁

Why do I feel this way?

_____

_____

_____

What can I do next week to feel great about money?

_____

_____

_____

# WEEK 7
## YOU ARE
## UNSTOPPABLE

# WEEKLY GOALS

### Goal #1

I am saving for

How much I need to save:

How will I reach my goal?

### Goal #2

I am saving for

How much I need to save:

How will I reach my goal?

### Goal #3

I am saving for

How much I need to save:

How will I reach my goal?

I attract money.

# DAY 43

**DATE:** _____

In one word, I feel: _____

I am grateful for: _____

Today's money affirmation statement:

_____

How I will work towards my weekly goals:

Goal #1: _____

Goal #2: _____

Goal #3: _____

---

Daily checklist:

◻ Review bank accounts    ◻ Review payments due
this week
◻ Review credit cards

◻ Pay bills that are due    ◻ _____

---

What did I spend money on today?

       Need    Want

_____ ◻    ◻

_____ ◻    ◻

_____ ◻    ◻

_____ ◻    ◻

_____ ◻    ◻

"I think everybody should get rich and famous and do everything they ever dreamed of so they can see that it's not the answer."

JIM CARREY

# DAY 44

**DATE:** _____

In one word, I feel: _____

I am grateful for: _____

Today's money affirmation statement:

_____

How I will work towards my weekly goals:

Goal #1: _____

Goal #2: _____

Goal #3: _____

Daily checklist:

☐ Review bank accounts          ☐ Review payments due
☐ Review credit cards              this week
☐ Pay bills that are due           ☐ _____

What did I spend money on today?

|  | Need | Want |
|---|---|---|
| _____ | ☐ | ☐ |
| _____ | ☐ | ☐ |
| _____ | ☐ | ☐ |
| _____ | ☐ | ☐ |
| _____ | ☐ | ☐ |

*"If you would be wealthy,
think of saving
as well as getting."*

Benjamin Franklin

Notes
_____
_____
_____
_____
_____
_____
_____
_____

# DAY 45

**DATE:** _____

In one word, I feel: _____

I am grateful for: _____

Today's money affirmation statement:

_____

How I will work towards my weekly goals:

Goal #1: _____

Goal #2: _____

Goal #3: _____

Daily checklist:
- ☐ Review bank accounts
- ☐ Review credit cards
- ☐ Pay bills that are due
- ☐ Review payments due this week
- ☐ _____

What did I spend money on today?

| | Need | Want |
|---|---|---|
| _____ | ☐ | ☐ |
| _____ | ☐ | ☐ |
| _____ | ☐ | ☐ |
| _____ | ☐ | ☐ |
| _____ | ☐ | ☐ |

I will attract and welcome more streams of income into my life.

Notes

# DAY 46

**DATE:** _____

In one word, I feel: _____

I am grateful for: _____

Today's money affirmation statement:

_____

How I will work towards my weekly goals:

Goal #1: _____

Goal #2: _____

Goal #3: _____

---

Daily checklist:

☐ Review bank accounts     ☐ Review payments due this week

☐ Review credit cards

☐ Pay bills that are due     ☐ _____

---

What did I spend money on today?

|  | Need | Want |
|---|---|---|
| _____ | ☐ | ☐ |
| _____ | ☐ | ☐ |
| _____ | ☐ | ☐ |
| _____ | ☐ | ☐ |
| _____ | ☐ | ☐ |

"Rich people have small TVs and big libraries, and poor people have small libraries and big TVs."

**Zig Ziglar**

# DAY 47

**DATE:** _____

In one word, I feel: _____

I am grateful for: _____

Today's money affirmation statement:

_____

How I will work towards my weekly goals:

Goal #1: _____

Goal #2: _____

Goal #3: _____

---

**Daily checklist:**

☐ Review bank accounts　　☐ Review payments due
this week

☐ Review credit cards

☐ Pay bills that are due　　☐ _____

---

## What did I spend money on today?

|  | Need | Want |
|---|---|---|
| _____ | ☐ | ☐ |
| _____ | ☐ | ☐ |
| _____ | ☐ | ☐ |
| _____ | ☐ | ☐ |
| _____ | ☐ | ☐ |

# I AM NOT AFRAID TO ASK FOR WHAT I AM WORTH.

Notes

# DAY 48

**DATE:** _____

In one word, I feel: _____

I am grateful for: _____

Today's money affirmation statement:

_____

How I will work towards my weekly goals:

Goal #1: _____

Goal #2: _____

Goal #3: _____

---

Daily checklist:

☐ Review bank accounts     ☐ Review payments due
☐ Review credit cards          this week
☐ Pay bills that are due      ☐ _____

---

What did I spend money on today?

|  | Need | Want |
|---|---|---|
| _____ | ☐ | ☐ |
| _____ | ☐ | ☐ |
| _____ | ☐ | ☐ |
| _____ | ☐ | ☐ |
| _____ | ☐ | ☐ |

"Money is only a tool. It will take you wherever you wish, but it will not replace you as the driver."

AYN RAND

Notes

# DAY 49

**DATE:**

In one word, I feel:

I am grateful for:

Today's money affirmation statement:

How I will work towards my weekly goals:

Goal #1:

Goal #2:

Goal #3:

Daily checklist:

- [ ] Review bank accounts
- [ ] Review credit cards
- [ ] Pay bills that are due
- [ ] Review payments due this week
- [ ]

What did I spend money on today?

| | Need | Want |
|---|---|---|
| | [ ] | [ ] |
| | [ ] | [ ] |
| | [ ] | [ ] |
| | [ ] | [ ] |
| | [ ] | [ ] |

# 10 MINUTE WEEKLY
# SELF - REFLECTION

In general, this week I feel:

Why do I feel this way?

_____

_____

_____

What can I do next week to feel great?

_____

_____

_____

# SELF - REFLECTION:  WEEK 7

This week I am the MOST grateful for:

_____

Something great that happened to me this week:

_____

How I feel about money this week:

🙁 ◯ ◯ ◯ ◯ 😐 ◯ ◯ ◯ ◯ 😁

Why do I feel this way?

_____

_____

_____

What can I do next week to feel great about money?

_____

_____

_____

# WEEK 8
## LET THE GOOD TIMES ROLL

# #NOBADDAYS

# WEEKLY GOALS

## Goal #1

I am saving for _____

How much I need to save: _____

How will I reach my goal? _____

_____

## Goal #2

I am saving for _____

How much I need to save: _____

How will I reach my goal? _____

_____

## Goal #3

I am saving for _____

How much I need to save: _____

How will I reach my goal? _____

_____

# "You can be young without money, but you can't be old without it."

TENNESSEE WILLIAMS

Notes

# DAY 50

**DATE:**

In one word, I feel:

I am grateful for:

Today's money affirmation statement:

How I will work towards my weekly goals:

Goal #1:

Goal #2:

Goal #3:

## Daily checklist:

☐ Review bank accounts
☐ Review credit cards
☐ Pay bills that are due
☐ Review payments due this week
☐

## What did I spend money on today?

| | Need | Want |
|---|---|---|
| | ☐ | ☐ |
| | ☐ | ☐ |
| | ☐ | ☐ |
| | ☐ | ☐ |
| | ☐ | ☐ |

I can and will have more than I ever dreamed possible.

# DAY 51

**DATE:** _____

In one word, I feel: _____

I am grateful for: _____

Today's money affirmation statement:

_____

How I will work towards my weekly goals:

Goal #1: _____

Goal #2: _____

Goal #3: _____

---

Daily checklist:

☐ Review bank accounts     ☐ Review payments due
this week
☐ Review credit cards

☐ Pay bills that are due     ☐ _____

---

What did I spend money on today?

|  | Need | Want |
|---|---|---|
| _____ | ☐ | ☐ |
| _____ | ☐ | ☐ |
| _____ | ☐ | ☐ |
| _____ | ☐ | ☐ |
| _____ | ☐ | ☐ |

"Don't let the fear of losing be greater than the excitement of winning."

ROBERT KIYOSAKI

Notes

# DAY 52

**DATE:**

In one word, I feel:

I am grateful for:

Today's money affirmation statement:

How I will work towards my weekly goals:

Goal #1:

Goal #2:

Goal #3:

**Daily checklist:**

- ☐ Review bank accounts
- ☐ Review credit cards
- ☐ Pay bills that are due
- ☐ Review payments due this week
- ☐

What did I spend money on today?

| | Need | Want |
|---|---|---|
| | ☐ | ☐ |
| | ☐ | ☐ |
| | ☐ | ☐ |
| | ☐ | ☐ |
| | ☐ | ☐ |

# I can afford it.

# DAY 53

**DATE:** _____

In one word, I feel: _____

I am grateful for: _____

Today's money affirmation statement:

_____

How I will work towards my weekly goals:

Goal #1: _____

Goal #2: _____

Goal #3: _____

---

Daily checklist:

☐ Review bank accounts
☐ Review credit cards
☐ Pay bills that are due

☐ Review payments due this week
☐ _____

---

What did I spend money on today?

|  | Need | Want |
|---|---|---|
| _____ | ☐ | ☐ |
| _____ | ☐ | ☐ |
| _____ | ☐ | ☐ |
| _____ | ☐ | ☐ |
| _____ | ☐ | ☐ |

# I am not a bad person for wanting more money.

# DAY 54

**DATE:**

In one word, I feel:

I am grateful for:

Today's money affirmation statement:

How I will work towards my weekly goals:

Goal #1:

Goal #2:

Goal #3:

## Daily checklist:

☐ Review bank accounts
☐ Review credit cards
☐ Pay bills that are due

☐ Review payments due this week
☐

What did I spend money on today?

| | Need | Want |
|---|---|---|
| | ☐ | ☐ |
| | ☐ | ☐ |
| | ☐ | ☐ |
| | ☐ | ☐ |
| | ☐ | ☐ |

I will continue to treat people the right way regardless of how much or how little money I have.

# DAY 55

**DATE:**

In one word, I feel:

I am grateful for:

Today's money affirmation statement:

How I will work towards my weekly goals:

Goal #1:

Goal #2:

Goal #3:

Daily checklist:

☐ Review bank accounts
☐ Review credit cards
☐ Pay bills that are due

☐ Review payments due this week
☐

What did I spend money on today?

| | Need | Want |
|---|---|---|
| | ☐ | ☐ |
| | ☐ | ☐ |
| | ☐ | ☐ |
| | ☐ | ☐ |
| | ☐ | ☐ |

"Success isn't measured by money or power or social rank. Success is measured by your discipline and inner peace."

MIKE DITKA

Notes

# DAY 56

**DATE:** _____

In one word, I feel: _____

I am grateful for: _____

Today's money affirmation statement:

_____

How I will work towards my weekly goals:

Goal #1: _____

Goal #2: _____

Goal #3: _____

---

Daily checklist:

- ☐ Review bank accounts
- ☐ Review credit cards
- ☐ Pay bills that are due
- ☐ Review payments due this week
- ☐ _____

---

What did I spend money on today?

| | Need | Want |
|---|---|---|
| _____ | ☐ | ☐ |
| _____ | ☐ | ☐ |
| _____ | ☐ | ☐ |
| _____ | ☐ | ☐ |
| _____ | ☐ | ☐ |

# 10 MINUTE WEEKLY SELF - REFLECTION

In general, this week I feel:

Why do I feel this way?

_____

_____

_____

What can I do next week to feel great?

_____

_____

_____

# SELF - REFLECTION:  WEEK 8

This week I am the MOST grateful for:

_____

Something great that happened to me this week:

_____

How I feel about money this week:

☹ ○ ○ ○ ○ 😐 ○ ○ ○ ○ 😁

Why do I feel this way?

_____

_____

_____

What can I do next week to feel great about money?

_____

_____

_____

# WEEK 9
## KEEP PUNCHING

"If you work hard in training,
the fight is easy."
- Manny Pacquiao.

# WEEKLY GOALS

### Goal #1

I am saving for ........................................................................

How much I need to save: ....................................

How will I reach my goal? .................................

........................................................................

### Goal #2

I am saving for ........................................................................

How much I need to save: ....................................

How will I reach my goal? .................................

........................................................................

### Goal #3

I am saving for ........................................................................

How much I need to save: ....................................

How will I reach my goal? .................................

........................................................................

"Empty pockets never held anyone back. Only empty heads and empty hearts can do that."

**NORMAN VINCENT PEALE**

Notes

# DAY 57

**DATE:**

In one word, I feel:

I am grateful for:

Today's money affirmation statement:

How I will work towards my weekly goals:

Goal #1:

Goal #2:

Goal #3:

Daily checklist:

- [ ] Review bank accounts
- [ ] Review credit cards
- [ ] Pay bills that are due
- [ ] Review payments due this week
- [ ]

What did I spend money on today?

| | Need | Want |
|---|---|---|
| | [ ] | [ ] |
| | [ ] | [ ] |
| | [ ] | [ ] |
| | [ ] | [ ] |
| | [ ] | [ ] |

# Money and love can co-exist in fruitful harmony.

# DAY 58

**DATE:** _____

In one word, I feel: _____

I am grateful for: _____

Today's money affirmation statement:

_____

How I will work towards my weekly goals:

Goal #1: _____

Goal #2: _____

Goal #3: _____

Daily checklist:

☐ Review bank accounts

☐ Review credit cards

☐ Pay bills that are due

☐ Review payments due this week

☐ _____

What did I spend money on today?

|  | Need | Want |
|---|:---:|:---:|
| _____ | ☐ | ☐ |
| _____ | ☐ | ☐ |
| _____ | ☐ | ☐ |
| _____ | ☐ | ☐ |
| _____ | ☐ | ☐ |

# My income is more than my expenses.

# DAY 59

**DATE:**

In one word, I feel:

I am grateful for:

Today's money affirmation statement:

How I will work towards my weekly goals:

Goal #1:

Goal #2:

Goal #3:

Daily checklist:

☐ Review bank accounts    ☐ Review payments due this week

☐ Review credit cards

☐ Pay bills that are due    ☐ _____

What did I spend money on today?

| | Need | Want |
|---|---|---|
| | ☐ | ☐ |
| | ☐ | ☐ |
| | ☐ | ☐ |
| | ☐ | ☐ |
| | ☐ | ☐ |

"Don't tell me what you value, show me your budget, and I'll tell you what you value."

JOE BIDEN

Notes

# DAY 60

**DATE:**_____

In one word, I feel: _____

I am grateful for: _____

Today's money affirmation statement:

_____

How I will work towards my weekly goals:

Goal #1: _____

Goal #2: _____

Goal #3: _____

---

Daily checklist:

☐ Review bank accounts      ☐ Review payments due this week

☐ Review credit cards

☐ Pay bills that are due      ☐ _____

---

What did I spend money on today?

| | Need | Want |
|---|---|---|
| _____ | ☐ | ☐ |
| _____ | ☐ | ☐ |
| _____ | ☐ | ☐ |
| _____ | ☐ | ☐ |
| _____ | ☐ | ☐ |

# "An investment in knowledge pays the best interest."

BENJAMIN FRANKLIN

Notes

# DAY 61

**DATE:**

In one word, I feel:

I am grateful for:

Today's money affirmation statement:

How I will work towards my weekly goals:

Goal #1:

Goal #2:

Goal #3:

Daily checklist:

- [ ] Review bank accounts
- [ ] Review credit cards
- [ ] Pay bills that are due
- [ ] Review payments due this week
- [ ]

What did I spend money on today?

| | Need | Want |
|---|---|---|
| | [ ] | [ ] |
| | [ ] | [ ] |
| | [ ] | [ ] |
| | [ ] | [ ] |
| | [ ] | [ ] |

# I create wealth and it is good for my family and I.

Notes

# DAY 62

**DATE:**

In one word, I feel:

I am grateful for:

Today's money affirmation statement:

How I will work towards my weekly goals:

Goal #1:

Goal #2:

Goal #3:

Daily checklist:

- [ ] Review bank accounts
- [ ] Review credit cards
- [ ] Pay bills that are due
- [ ] Review payments due this week
- [ ]

What did I spend money on today?

| | Need | Want |
|---|---|---|
| | [ ] | [ ] |
| | [ ] | [ ] |
| | [ ] | [ ] |
| | [ ] | [ ] |
| | [ ] | [ ] |

**"You must gain control over your money or the lack of it will forever control you."**

Dave Ramsey

# DAY 63

**DATE:**

In one word, I feel:

I am grateful for:

Today's money affirmation statement:

How I will work towards my weekly goals:

Goal #1:

Goal #2:

Goal #3:

Daily checklist:

☐ Review bank accounts

☐ Review credit cards

☐ Pay bills that are due

☐ Review payments due this week

☐ _____

What did I spend money on today?

| | Need | Want |
|---|---|---|
| | ☐ | ☐ |
| | ☐ | ☐ |
| | ☐ | ☐ |
| | ☐ | ☐ |
| | ☐ | ☐ |

# 10 MINUTE WEEKLY
# SELF - REFLECTION

In general, this week I feel:

Why do I feel this way?

_____

_____

_____

What can I do next week to feel great?

_____

_____

_____

# SELF - REFLECTION: WEEK 9

This week I am the MOST grateful for:

_____

Something great that happened to me this week:

_____

How I feel about money this week:

😕 ⚪ ⚪ ⚪ ⚪ 😐 ⚪ ⚪ ⚪ ⚪ 😁

Why do I feel this way?

_____

_____

_____

What can I do next week to feel great about money?

_____

_____

_____

# WEEK 10
## GRATITUDE IS THE ATTITUDE

The answer to many of life's problems is gratitude.

# WEEKLY GOALS

## Goal #1

I am saving for _____

How much I need to save: _____

How will I reach my goal? _____

_____

## Goal #2

I am saving for _____

How much I need to save: _____

How will I reach my goal? _____

_____

## Goal #3

I am saving for _____

How much I need to save: _____

How will I reach my goal? _____

_____

"Don't tell me where your priorities are. Show me where you spend your money and I'll tell you what they are."

James W. Frick

# DAY 64

**DATE:** _____

In one word, I feel: _____

I am grateful for: _____

Today's money affirmation statement:

_____

How I will work towards my weekly goals:

Goal #1: _____

Goal #2: _____

Goal #3: _____

---

Daily checklist:

☐ Review bank accounts     ☐ Review payments due this week

☐ Review credit cards

☐ Pay bills that are due     ☐ _____

---

What did I spend money on today?

|  | Need | Want |
|---|---|---|
| _____ | ☐ | ☐ |
| _____ | ☐ | ☐ |
| _____ | ☐ | ☐ |
| _____ | ☐ | ☐ |
| _____ | ☐ | ☐ |

I am open to giving money to support people in less fortunate situations.

# DAY 65

**DATE:**

In one word, I feel:

I am grateful for:

Today's money affirmation statement:

How I will work towards my weekly goals:

Goal #1:

Goal #2:

Goal #3:

Daily checklist:

☐ Review bank accounts

☐ Review credit cards

☐ Pay bills that are due

☐ Review payments due this week

☐

What did I spend money on today?

| | Need | Want |
|---|---|---|
| | ☐ | ☐ |
| | ☐ | ☐ |
| | ☐ | ☐ |
| | ☐ | ☐ |
| | ☐ | ☐ |

# PROSPERITY WILL COME TO ME AND I WILL FULLY EMBRACE IT WHEN IT COMES.

Notes

# DAY 66

**DATE:** _____

In one word, I feel: _____

I am grateful for: _____

Today's money affirmation statement:

_____

How I will work towards my weekly goals:

Goal #1: _____

Goal #2: _____

Goal #3: _____

---

Daily checklist:

☐ Review bank accounts      ☐ Review payments due
                              this week
☐ Review credit cards
                            ☐ _____
☐ Pay bills that are due

---

What did I spend money on today?

|  | Need | Want |
|---|---|---|
| _____ | ☐ | ☐ |
| _____ | ☐ | ☐ |
| _____ | ☐ | ☐ |
| _____ | ☐ | ☐ |
| _____ | ☐ | ☐ |

"Financial peace isn't the acquisition of stuff. It's learning to live on less than you make, so you can give money back and have money to invest. You can't win until you do this."

Dave Ramsey

Notes

# DAY 67

**DATE:**

In one word, I feel:

I am grateful for:

Today's money affirmation statement:

How I will work towards my weekly goals:

Goal #1:

Goal #2:

Goal #3:

## Daily checklist:

- [ ] Review bank accounts
- [ ] Review credit cards
- [ ] Pay bills that are due
- [ ] Review payments due this week
- [ ]

## What did I spend money on today?

| | Need | Want |
|---|---|---|
| | [ ] | [ ] |
| | [ ] | [ ] |
| | [ ] | [ ] |
| | [ ] | [ ] |
| | [ ] | [ ] |

"Money is numbers and numbers never end. If it takes money to be happy, your search for happiness will never end."

Bob Marley

# DAY 68

**DATE:** _____

In one word, I feel: _____

I am grateful for: _____

Today's money affirmation statement:

_____

How I will work towards my weekly goals:

Goal #1: _____

Goal #2: _____

Goal #3: _____

---

Daily checklist:

☐ Review bank accounts    ☐ Review payments due this week

☐ Review credit cards

☐ Pay bills that are due    ☐ _____

---

What did I spend money on today?

| | Need | Want |
|---|---|---|
| _____ | ☐ | ☐ |
| _____ | ☐ | ☐ |
| _____ | ☐ | ☐ |
| _____ | ☐ | ☐ |
| _____ | ☐ | ☐ |

# Wealth constantly flows into my life.

Notes

# DAY 69

**DATE:**

In one word, I feel:

I am grateful for:

Today's money affirmation statement:

How I will work towards my weekly goals:

Goal #1:

Goal #2:

Goal #3:

Daily checklist:

☐ Review bank accounts   ☐ Review payments due
                          this week
☐ Review credit cards
                          ☐
☐ Pay bills that are due

What did I spend money on today?

|  | Need | Want |
|---|---|---|
|  | ☐ | ☐ |
|  | ☐ | ☐ |
|  | ☐ | ☐ |
|  | ☐ | ☐ |
|  | ☐ | ☐ |

"If you're saving, you're succeeding."

*STEVE BURKHOLDER*

Notes

# DAY 70

**DATE:** _____

In one word, I feel: _____

I am grateful for: _____

Today's money affirmation statement:

_____

How I will work towards my weekly goals:

Goal #1: _____

Goal #2: _____

Goal #3: _____

---

Daily checklist:

☐ Review bank accounts　　☐ Review payments due this week

☐ Review credit cards

☐ Pay bills that are due　　☐ _____

---

What did I spend money on today?

| | Need | Want |
|---|---|---|
| _____ | ☐ | ☐ |
| _____ | ☐ | ☐ |
| _____ | ☐ | ☐ |
| _____ | ☐ | ☐ |
| _____ | ☐ | ☐ |

# 10 MINUTE WEEKLY SELF - REFLECTION

In general, this week I feel:

Why do I feel this way?

_____

_____

_____

What can I do next week to feel great?

_____

_____

_____

# SELF - REFLECTION: WEEK 10

This week I am the MOST grateful for:

_____

Something great that happened to me this week:

_____

How I feel about money this week:

😕 ◯ ◯ ◯ ◯ 😐 ◯ ◯ ◯ ◯ 😁

Why do I feel this way?

_____

_____

_____

What can I do next week to feel great about money?

_____

_____

_____

# WEEK 11
## STAY FOCUSED

*Feed your focus, starve your distractions.*

# WEEKLY GOALS

## Goal #1

I am saving for _____

How much I need to save: _____

How will I reach my goal? _____

_____

## Goal #2

I am saving for _____

How much I need to save: _____

How will I reach my goal? _____

_____

## Goal #3

I am saving for _____

How much I need to save: _____

How will I reach my goal? _____

_____

"Many folks think they aren't good at earning money when what they don't know is how to use it."

FRANK A. CLARK

Notes

# DAY 71

**DATE:**

In one word, I feel:

I am grateful for:

Today's money affirmation statement:

How I will work towards my weekly goals:

Goal #1:

Goal #2:

Goal #3:

Daily checklist:

☐ Review bank accounts
☐ Review credit cards
☐ Pay bills that are due

☐ Review payments due this week
☐ _____

What did I spend money on today?

|  | Need | Want |
|---|---|---|
|  | ☐ | ☐ |
|  | ☐ | ☐ |
|  | ☐ | ☐ |
|  | ☐ | ☐ |
|  | ☐ | ☐ |

*I will always have everything that I need.*

Notes

# DAY 72

**DATE:** _____

In one word, I feel: _____

I am grateful for: _____

Today's money affirmation statement:

_____

How I will work towards my weekly goals:

Goal #1: _____

Goal #2: _____

Goal #3: _____

---

Daily checklist:

☐ Review bank accounts     ☐ Review payments due
                              this week
☐ Review credit cards
                            ☐ _____
☐ Pay bills that are due

---

What did I spend money on today?

|  | Need | Want |
|---|---|---|
| _____ | ☐ | ☐ |
| _____ | ☐ | ☐ |
| _____ | ☐ | ☐ |
| _____ | ☐ | ☐ |
| _____ | ☐ | ☐ |

Instead of "I can't afford it",
let's try "how can I afford it?"

# DAY 73

**DATE:** _____

In one word, I feel: _____

I am grateful for: _____

Today's money affirmation statement:

_____

How I will work towards my weekly goals:

Goal #1: _____

Goal #2: _____

Goal #3: _____

---

Daily checklist:

☐ Review bank accounts  ☐ Review payments due
☐ Review credit cards      this week
☐ Pay bills that are due  ☐ _____

---

What did I spend money on today?

|  | Need | Want |
|---|---|---|
| _____ | ☐ | ☐ |
| _____ | ☐ | ☐ |
| _____ | ☐ | ☐ |
| _____ | ☐ | ☐ |
| _____ | ☐ | ☐ |

# "WEALTH IS THE ABILITY TO FULLY EXPERIENCE LIFE."

HENRY DAVID THOREAU

# DAY 74

**DATE:**

In one word, I feel:

I am grateful for:

Today's money affirmation statement:

How I will work towards my weekly goals:

Goal #1:

Goal #2:

Goal #3:

Daily checklist:

☐ Review bank accounts
☐ Review credit cards
☐ Pay bills that are due

☐ Review payments due this week
☐

What did I spend money on today?

|  | Need | Want |
|---|---|---|
|  | ☐ | ☐ |
|  | ☐ | ☐ |
|  | ☐ | ☐ |
|  | ☐ | ☐ |
|  | ☐ | ☐ |

# I will always have more than enough money.

## Notes

# DAY 75

**DATE:** _____

In one word, I feel: _____

I am grateful for: _____

Today's money affirmation statement:

_____

How I will work towards my weekly goals:

Goal #1: _____

Goal #2: _____

Goal #3: _____

---

Daily checklist:

☐ Review bank accounts       ☐ Review payments due
☐ Review credit cards            this week
☐ Pay bills that are due       ☐ _____

---

What did I spend money on today?

|  | Need | Want |
|---|---|---|
| _____ | ☐ | ☐ |
| _____ | ☐ | ☐ |
| _____ | ☐ | ☐ |
| _____ | ☐ | ☐ |
| _____ | ☐ | ☐ |

*"Invest in as much of yourself as you can, you are your own biggest asset by far."*

Warren Buffett

# DAY 76

**DATE:** _____

In one word, I feel: _____

I am grateful for: _____

Today's money affirmation statement:

_____

How I will work towards my weekly goals:

Goal #1: _____

Goal #2: _____

Goal #3: _____

---

Daily checklist:

☐ Review bank accounts    ☐ Review payments due this week

☐ Review credit cards

☐ Pay bills that are due    ☐ _____

---

What did I spend money on today?

| | Need | Want |
|---|---|---|
| _____ | ☐ | ☐ |
| _____ | ☐ | ☐ |
| _____ | ☐ | ☐ |
| _____ | ☐ | ☐ |
| _____ | ☐ | ☐ |

Most wealth is inconspicuous. The man down the street driving the nice car and living in the mansion could easily have greater debt and a lower net worth than the stealthy and wealthy plumber who drives a beat-up truck but seems to work only when he doesn't feel like fishing.

LORAL LANGEMEIER

Notes

# DAY 77

**DATE:**_____

In one word, I feel: _____

I am grateful for: _____

Today's money affirmation statement:

_____

How I will work towards my weekly goals:

Goal #1: _____

Goal #2: _____

Goal #3: _____

---

Daily checklist:

☐ Review bank accounts    ☐ Review payments due this week

☐ Review credit cards

☐ Pay bills that are due    ☐ _____

---

What did I spend money on today?

|  | Need | Want |
|---|---|---|
| _____ | ☐ | ☐ |
| _____ | ☐ | ☐ |
| _____ | ☐ | ☐ |
| _____ | ☐ | ☐ |
| _____ | ☐ | ☐ |

# 10 MINUTE WEEKLY
# SELF - REFLECTION

In general, this week I feel:

Why do I feel this way?

_____

_____

_____

What can I do next week to feel great?

_____

_____

_____

# SELF - REFLECTION:  WEEK 11

This week I am the MOST grateful for:

_____

Something great that happened to me this week:

_____

How I feel about money this week:

😕 ◯ ◯ ◯ ◯ 😐 ◯ ◯ ◯ ◯ 😁

Why do I feel this way?

_____

_____

_____

What can I do next week to feel great about money?

_____

_____

_____

# WEEK 12
## KEEP SHINING

# WEEKLY GOALS

## Goal #1

I am saving for _____

How much I need to save: _____

How will I reach my goal? _____

_____

## Goal #2

I am saving for _____

How much I need to save: _____

How will I reach my goal? _____

_____

## Goal #3

I am saving for _____

How much I need to save: _____

How will I reach my goal? _____

_____

# I am financially free.

# DAY 78

**DATE:**

In one word, I feel:

I am grateful for:

Today's money affirmation statement:

How I will work towards my weekly goals:

Goal #1:

Goal #2:

Goal #3:

Daily checklist:

- [ ] Review bank accounts
- [ ] Review credit cards
- [ ] Pay bills that are due
- [ ] Review payments due this week
- [ ]

What did I spend money on today?

| | Need | Want |
|---|---|---|
| | [ ] | [ ] |
| | [ ] | [ ] |
| | [ ] | [ ] |
| | [ ] | [ ] |
| | [ ] | [ ] |

"You can change your health, you can change your relationships, you can change your income, you can change anything."

BOB PROCTOR

# DAY 79

**DATE:**_____

n one word, I feel: _____

am grateful for: _____

Today's money affirmation statement:

_____

How I will work towards my weekly goals:

Goal #1: _____

Goal #2: _____

Goal #3: _____

---

Daily checklist:

☐ Review bank accounts    ☐ Review payments due
this week

☐ Review credit cards

☐ Pay bills that are due    ☐ _____

---

What did I spend money on today?

| | Need | Want |
|---|---|---|
| _____ | ☐ | ☐ |
| _____ | ☐ | ☐ |
| _____ | ☐ | ☐ |
| _____ | ☐ | ☐ |
| _____ | ☐ | ☐ |

*I believe in my ability to earn the income that I desire.*

# DAY 80

**DATE:** _____

In one word, I feel: _____

I am grateful for: _____

Today's money affirmation statement:

_____

How I will work towards my weekly goals:

Goal #1: _____

Goal #2: _____

Goal #3: _____

Daily checklist:

☐ Review bank accounts        ☐ Review payments due
☐ Review credit cards              this week
☐ Pay bills that are due          ☐ _____

What did I spend money on today?

|  | Need | Want |
|---|---|---|
| _____ | ☐ | ☐ |
| _____ | ☐ | ☐ |
| _____ | ☐ | ☐ |
| _____ | ☐ | ☐ |
| _____ | ☐ | ☐ |

"formal education will make you a living; self-education will make you a fortune."

Jim Rohn

# DAY 81

**DATE:**

In one word, I feel:

I am grateful for:

Today's money affirmation statement:

How I will work towards my weekly goals:

Goal #1:

Goal #2:

Goal #3:

Daily checklist:

☐ Review bank accounts
☐ Review credit cards
☐ Pay bills that are due

☐ Review payments due this week

☐

What did I spend money on today?

| | Need | Want |
|---|---|---|
| | ☐ | ☐ |
| | ☐ | ☐ |
| | ☐ | ☐ |
| | ☐ | ☐ |
| | ☐ | ☐ |

# If you dreams don't scare you, they aren't big enough.

# DAY 82

**DATE:**

In one word, I feel:

I am grateful for:

Today's money affirmation statement:

How I will work towards my weekly goals:

Goal #1:

Goal #2:

Goal #3:

Daily checklist:

- [ ] Review bank accounts
- [ ] Review credit cards
- [ ] Pay bills that are due
- [ ] Review payments due this week
- [ ]

What did I spend money on today?

| | Need | Want |
|---|---|---|
| | [ ] | [ ] |
| | [ ] | [ ] |
| | [ ] | [ ] |
| | [ ] | [ ] |
| | [ ] | [ ] |

# "IF YOU CANNOT CONTROL YOUR EMOTIONS, YOU CANNOT CONTROL YOUR MONEY."

Warren Buffett

Notes

# DAY 83

**DATE:** _____

In one word, I feel: _____

I am grateful for: _____

Today's money affirmation statement:

_____

How I will work towards my weekly goals:

Goal #1: _____

Goal #2: _____

Goal #3: _____

---

Daily checklist:

☐ Review bank accounts
☐ Review credit cards
☐ Pay bills that are due

☐ Review payments due this week
☐ _____

---

What did I spend money on today?

|  | Need | Want |
|---|---|---|
| _____ | ☐ | ☐ |
| _____ | ☐ | ☐ |
| _____ | ☐ | ☐ |
| _____ | ☐ | ☐ |
| _____ | ☐ | ☐ |

"You can only become truly accomplished at something you love. Don't make money your goal.

Instead, pursue the things you love doing, and then do them so well that people can't take their eyes off you."

MAYA ANGELOU

Notes

# DAY 84

**DATE:** _____

In one word, I feel: _____

I am grateful for: _____

Today's money affirmation statement:

_____

How I will work towards my weekly goals:

Goal #1: _____

Goal #2: _____

Goal #3: _____

---

Daily checklist:

☐ Review bank accounts　　☐ Review payments due
☐ Review credit cards　　　　this week
☐ Pay bills that are due　　☐ _____

---

What did I spend money on today?

| | Need | Want |
|---|---|---|
| _____ | ☐ | ☐ |
| _____ | ☐ | ☐ |
| _____ | ☐ | ☐ |
| _____ | ☐ | ☐ |
| _____ | ☐ | ☐ |

# 10 MINUTE WEEKLY SELF - REFLECTION

In general, this week I feel:

Why do I feel this way?

_____

_____

_____

What can I do next week to feel great?

_____

_____

_____

# SELF - REFLECTION:  WEEK 12

This week I am the MOST grateful for:

_____

Something great that happened to me this week:

_____

How I feel about money this week:

☹ ○ ○ ○ ○ 😐 ○ ○ ○ ○ 😃

Why do I feel this way?

_____

_____

_____

What can I do next week to feel great about money?

_____

_____

_____

# WEEK 13
## UNLIMITED
## POTENTIAL

*Grab some shades,*
*Your future is bright!*

# WEEKLY GOALS

### Goal #1

I am saving for _____

How much I need to save: _____

How will I reach my goal? _____

_____

### Goal #2

I am saving for _____

How much I need to save: _____

How will I reach my goal? _____

_____

### Goal #3

I am saving for _____

How much I need to save: _____

How will I reach my goal? _____

_____

"If we command our wealth, we shall be rich and free. If our wealth commands us, we are poor indeed."

EDMUND BURKE

Notes

# DAY 85

**DATE:** _____

In one word, I feel: _____

I am grateful for: _____

Today's money affirmation statement:

_____

How I will work towards my weekly goals:

Goal #1: _____

Goal #2: _____

Goal #3: _____

---

Daily checklist:

☐ Review bank accounts    ☐ Review payments due this week

☐ Review credit cards

☐ Pay bills that are due    ☐ _____

---

What did I spend money on today?

|  | Need | Want |
|---|---|---|
| _____ | ☐ | ☐ |
| _____ | ☐ | ☐ |
| _____ | ☐ | ☐ |
| _____ | ☐ | ☐ |
| _____ | ☐ | ☐ |

I respect that money is an exchange of energy and that it needs to flow and move.

# DAY 86

**DATE:** _____

In one word, I feel: _____

I am grateful for: _____

Today's money affirmation statement:

_____

How I will work towards my weekly goals:

Goal #1: _____

Goal #2: _____

Goal #3: _____

Daily checklist:

☐ Review bank accounts

☐ Review credit cards

☐ Pay bills that are due

☐ Review payments due this week

☐ _____

What did I spend money on today?

|  | Need | Want |
|---|---|---|
| _____ | ☐ | ☐ |
| _____ | ☐ | ☐ |
| _____ | ☐ | ☐ |
| _____ | ☐ | ☐ |
| _____ | ☐ | ☐ |

"Investing should be more like watching paint dry or watching grass grow. If you want excitement, take $800 and go to Las Vegas."

PAUL SAMUELSON

Notes

# DAY 87

**DATE:** _____

In one word, I feel: _____

I am grateful for: _____

Today's money affirmation statement:

_____

How I will work towards my weekly goals:

Goal #1: _____

Goal #2: _____

Goal #3: _____

---

Daily checklist:

☐ Review bank accounts    ☐ Review payments due this week

☐ Review credit cards

☐ Pay bills that are due    ☐ _____

---

What did I spend money on today?

|  | Need | Want |
|---|:---:|:---:|
| _____ | ☐ | ☐ |
| _____ | ☐ | ☐ |
| _____ | ☐ | ☐ |
| _____ | ☐ | ☐ |
| _____ | ☐ | ☐ |

# I am confident and able to create more wealth in my life.

Notes

# DAY 88

**DATE:** _____

In one word, I feel: _____

I am grateful for: _____

Today's money affirmation statement:

_____

How I will work towards my weekly goals:

Goal #1: _____

Goal #2: _____

Goal #3: _____

---

Daily checklist:

☐ Review bank accounts     ☐ Review payments due this week

☐ Review credit cards

☐ Pay bills that are due     ☐ _____

---

What did I spend money on today?

|  | Need | Want |
|---|---|---|
| _____ | ☐ | ☐ |
| _____ | ☐ | ☐ |
| _____ | ☐ | ☐ |
| _____ | ☐ | ☐ |
| _____ | ☐ | ☐ |

# It's not how much money you make, but how much money you keep, how hard it works for you, and how many generations you keep it for.

Robert Kiyosaki

Notes

# DAY 89

**DATE:**_____

In one word, I feel: _____

I am grateful for: _____

Today's money affirmation statement:

_____

How I will work towards my weekly goals:

Goal #1: _____

Goal #2: _____

Goal #3: _____

---

Daily checklist:

☐ Review bank accounts    ☐ Review payments due
this week
☐ Review credit cards
☐ Pay bills that are due    ☐ _____

---

What did I spend money on today?

|  | Need | Want |
|---|---|---|
| _____ | ☐ | ☐ |
| _____ | ☐ | ☐ |
| _____ | ☐ | ☐ |
| _____ | ☐ | ☐ |
| _____ | ☐ | ☐ |

My bank account
has enough and
I am happy.

Notes

# DAY 90

**DATE:** _____

In one word, I feel: _____

I am grateful for: _____

Today's money affirmation statement:

_____

How I will work towards my weekly goals:

Goal #1: _____

Goal #2: _____

Goal #3: _____

---

Daily checklist:

☐ Review bank accounts        ☐ Review payments due
                                this week
☐ Review credit cards
                              ☐ _____
☐ Pay bills that are due

---

What did I spend money on today?

|  | Need | Want |
|---|---|---|
| _____ | ☐ | ☐ |
| _____ | ☐ | ☐ |
| _____ | ☐ | ☐ |
| _____ | ☐ | ☐ |
| _____ | ☐ | ☐ |

"It's good to have money and the things that money can buy, but it's good, too, to check up once in a while and make sure that you haven't lost the things that money can't buy."

GEORGE LORIMER

Notes

# DAY 91

**DATE:** _____

In one word, I feel: _____

I am grateful for: _____

Today's money affirmation statement:

_____

How I will work towards my weekly goals:

Goal #1: _____

Goal #2: _____

Goal #3: _____

---

Daily checklist:

☐ Review bank accounts    ☐ Review payments due this week

☐ Review credit cards

☐ Pay bills that are due    ☐ _____

---

What did I spend money on today?

| | Need | Want |
|---|---|---|
| _____ | ☐ | ☐ |
| _____ | ☐ | ☐ |
| _____ | ☐ | ☐ |
| _____ | ☐ | ☐ |
| _____ | ☐ | ☐ |

# 10 MINUTE WEEKLY SELF - REFLECTION

In general, this week I feel:

😕 ○ ○ ○ ○ 😐 ○ ○ ○ ○ 😄

Why do I feel this way?

_____

_____

_____

What can I do next week to feel great?

_____

_____

_____

# SELF - REFLECTION:  WEEK 13

This week I am the MOST grateful for:

_____

Something great that happened to me this week:

_____

How I feel about money this week:

😕 ⚪ ⚪ ⚪ ⚪ 😐 ⚪ ⚪ ⚪ ⚪ 😁

Why do I feel this way?

_____

_____

_____

What can I do next week to feel great about money?

_____

_____

_____

# WEEK 14
## HOME STRETCH

*It always seems impossible until it's done.*

# WEEKLY GOALS

## Goal #1

I am saving for _____

How much I need to save: _____

How will I reach my goal? _____

_____

## Goal #2

I am saving for _____

How much I need to save: _____

How will I reach my goal? _____

_____

## Goal #3

I am saving for _____

How much I need to save: _____

How will I reach my goal? _____

_____

"Money moves from those who do not manage it to those who do."

**DAVE RAMSEY**

# DAY 92

**DATE:**

In one word, I feel:

I am grateful for:

Today's money affirmation statement:

How I will work towards my weekly goals:

Goal #1:

Goal #2:

Goal #3:

Daily checklist:

☐ Review bank accounts
☐ Review credit cards
☐ Pay bills that are due

☐ Review payments due this week
☐

What did I spend money on today?

| | Need | Want |
|---|---|---|
| | ☐ | ☐ |
| | ☐ | ☐ |
| | ☐ | ☐ |
| | ☐ | ☐ |
| | ☐ | ☐ |

# I will actively remove barriers and negative thoughts about money.

Notes

# DAY 93

**DATE:**

In one word, I feel:

I am grateful for:

Today's money affirmation statement:

How I will work towards my weekly goals:

Goal #1:

Goal #2:

Goal #3:

Daily checklist:

☐ Review bank accounts
☐ Review credit cards
☐ Pay bills that are due

☐ Review payments due this week
☐

What did I spend money on today?

| | Need | Want |
|---|---|---|
| | ☐ | ☐ |
| | ☐ | ☐ |
| | ☐ | ☐ |
| | ☐ | ☐ |
| | ☐ | ☐ |

# I will give first, take last.

# DAY 94

**DATE:** _____

In one word, I feel: _____

I am grateful for: _____

Today's money affirmation statement:

_____

How I will work towards my weekly goals:

Goal #1: _____

Goal #2: _____

Goal #3: _____

---

Daily checklist:

☐ Review bank accounts    ☐ Review payments due this week

☐ Review credit cards

☐ Pay bills that are due    ☐ _____

---

What did I spend money on today?

| | Need | Want |
|---|---|---|
| _____ | ☐ | ☐ |
| _____ | ☐ | ☐ |
| _____ | ☐ | ☐ |
| _____ | ☐ | ☐ |
| _____ | ☐ | ☐ |

"Spend your money on the things money can buy. Spend your time on the things money can't buy."

HARUKI MURAKAMI

Notes

# DAY 95

**DATE:** _____

In one word, I feel: _____

I am grateful for: _____

Today's money affirmation statement:

_____

How I will work towards my weekly goals:

Goal #1: _____

Goal #2: _____

Goal #3: _____

---

Daily checklist:

☐ Review bank accounts    ☐ Review payments due
☐ Review credit cards          this week
☐ Pay bills that are due    ☐ _____

---

What did I spend money on today?

| | Need | Want |
|---|---|---|
| _____ | ☐ | ☐ |
| _____ | ☐ | ☐ |
| _____ | ☐ | ☐ |
| _____ | ☐ | ☐ |
| _____ | ☐ | ☐ |

# Wealth and abundance are energies that I am aligned with.

# DAY 96

**DATE:** _____

In one word, I feel: _____

I am grateful for: _____

Today's money affirmation statement:

_____

How I will work towards my weekly goals:

Goal #1: _____

Goal #2: _____

Goal #3: _____

Daily checklist:

☐ Review bank accounts    ☐ Review payments due this week

☐ Review credit cards

☐ Pay bills that are due    ☐ _____

What did I spend money on today?

| | Need | Want |
|---|---|---|
| _____ | ☐ | ☐ |
| _____ | ☐ | ☐ |
| _____ | ☐ | ☐ |
| _____ | ☐ | ☐ |
| _____ | ☐ | ☐ |

## "You will attract everything that you require..."

Bob Proctor

# DAY 97

**DATE:** _____

In one word, I feel: _____

I am grateful for: _____

Today's money affirmation statement:

_____

How I will work towards my weekly goals:

Goal #1: _____

Goal #2: _____

Goal #3: _____

Daily checklist:

☐ Review bank accounts    ☐ Review payments due this week

☐ Review credit cards

☐ Pay bills that are due    ☐ _____

What did I spend money on today?

|  | Need | Want |
|---|---|---|
| _____ | ☐ | ☐ |
| _____ | ☐ | ☐ |
| _____ | ☐ | ☐ |
| _____ | ☐ | ☐ |
| _____ | ☐ | ☐ |

# "Trade money for time, not time for money. You're going to run out of time first."

Naval Ravikant

# DAY 98

**DATE:** _____

In one word, I feel: _____

I am grateful for: _____

Today's money affirmation statement:

_____

How I will work towards my weekly goals:

Goal #1: _____

Goal #2: _____

Goal #3: _____

Daily checklist:

☐ Review bank accounts          ☐ Review payments due
☐ Review credit cards              this week
☐ Pay bills that are due          ☐ _____

What did I spend money on today?

|  | Need | Want |
|---|---|---|
| _____ | ☐ | ☐ |
| _____ | ☐ | ☐ |
| _____ | ☐ | ☐ |
| _____ | ☐ | ☐ |
| _____ | ☐ | ☐ |

# 10 MINUTE WEEKLY SELF - REFLECTION

In general, this week I feel:

Why do I feel this way?

_____

_____

_____

What can I do next week to feel great?

_____

_____

_____

# SELF - REFLECTION:  WEEK 14

This week I am the MOST grateful for:

_____

Something great that happened to me this week:

_____

How I feel about money this week:

😟 ◯ ◯ ◯ ◯ 😐 ◯ ◯ ◯ ◯ 😁

Why do I feel this way?

_____

_____

_____

What can I do next week to feel great about money?

_____

_____

_____

# WEEK 15
## TWO.
## MORE.
## DAYS.

*Celebrate your wins*

# WEEKLY GOALS

## Goal #1

I am saving for _____

How much I need to save: _____

How will I reach my goal? _____

_____

## Goal #2

I am saving for _____

How much I need to save: _____

How will I reach my goal? _____

_____

## Goal #3

I am saving for _____

How much I need to save: _____

How will I reach my goal? _____

_____

# Don't go broke trying to look rich.

# DAY 99

**DATE:** _____

In one word, I feel: _____

I am grateful for: _____

Today's money affirmation statement:

_____

How I will work towards my weekly goals:

Goal #1: _____

Goal #2: _____

Goal #3: _____

---

Daily checklist:

☐ Review bank accounts    ☐ Review payments due this week

☐ Review credit cards

☐ Pay bills that are due    ☐ _____

---

## What did I spend money on today?

|  | Need | Want |
|---|---|---|
| _____ | ☐ | ☐ |
| _____ | ☐ | ☐ |
| _____ | ☐ | ☐ |
| _____ | ☐ | ☐ |
| _____ | ☐ | ☐ |

"Too many people spend money they haven't earned to buy things they don't want to impress people they don't like."

Will Rogers

# DAY 100

**DATE:** _____

In one word, I feel: _____

I am grateful for: _____

Today's money affirmation statement:

_____

How I will work towards my weekly goals:

Goal #1: _____

Goal #2: _____

Goal #3: _____

Daily checklist:

☐ Review bank accounts   ☐ Review payments due
☐ Review credit cards        this week
☐ Pay bills that are due   ☐ _____

What did I spend money on today?

|  | Need | Want |
|---|---|---|
| _____ | ☐ | ☐ |
| _____ | ☐ | ☐ |
| _____ | ☐ | ☐ |
| _____ | ☐ | ☐ |
| _____ | ☐ | ☐ |

# 100 DAY MONEY JOURNAL SELF - REFLECTION

After completing 100 days of journalling, I feel:

I dedicated 100% effort to this money journal:

My goals were realistic and achievable:

I consistently achieved my money goals:

How I feel about my financial situation:

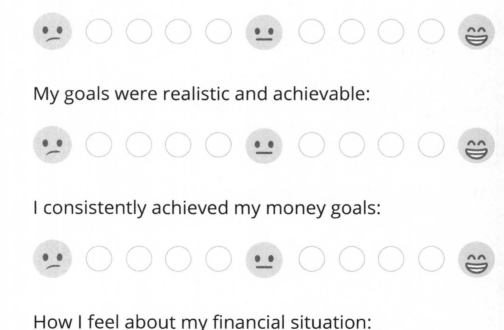

# SELF - REFLECTION

Key things I learned during this 100 day period:

_____

_____

_____

_____

_____

How I feel about my money mindset:

🙁 ○ ○ ○ ○ 😐 ○ ○ ○ ○ 😁

I will continue to improve my money mindset by:

_____

_____

_____

My upcoming financial goals:

_____

_____

_____

_____

# MY FAVORITE
## money affirmations

# MY FAVORITE
## money affirmations

# NOTES

# NOTES

# NOTES

# NOTES

# NOTES

# NOTES

# NOTES

# NOTES

# NOTES

# NOTES